SUPER SIMPLE
FOREST
CRITTER CRAFTS

Fun and Easy Animal Crafts

Alex Kuskowski

Consulting Editor, Diane Craig, M.A./Reading Specialist

Super Sandcastle

An Imprint of Abdo Publishing
abdopublishing.com

abdopublishing.com

Published by Abdo Publishing, a division of ABDO, PO Box 398166, Minneapolis, Minnesota 55439. Copyright © 2017 by Abdo Consulting Group, Inc. International copyrights reserved in all countries. No part of this book may be reproduced in any form without written permission from the publisher. Super SandCastle™ is a trademark and logo of Abdo Publishing.

Printed in the United States of America, North Mankato, Minnesota
062016
092016

Editor: Liz Salzmann
Content Developer: Nancy Tuminelly
Craft Production: Frankie Tuminelly
Cover and Interior Design and Production: Colleen Dolphin, Mighty Media, Inc.
Photo Credits: Mighty Media, Inc.; Shutterstock
The following manufacturers/names appearing in this book are trademarks:
Scribbles®, Sharpie®

Library of Congress Cataloging-in-Publication Data
Names: Kuskowski, Alex, author.
Title: Super simple forest critter crafts : fun and easy animal crafts / by
   Alex Kuskowski ; consulting editor, Diane Craig, M.A./reading specialist.
Description: Minneapolis, Minnesota : Abdo Publishing, [2017] | Series:
   Super simple critter crafts
Identifiers: LCCN 2016000308 (print) | LCCN 2016002047 (ebook) | ISBN
   9781680781625 (print) | ISBN 9781680776058 (ebook)
Subjects: LCSH: Handicraft--Juvenile literature. | Forest animals--Juvenile
   literature.
Classification: LCC TT160 .K874254 2017 (print) | LCC TT160 (ebook) | DDC
   745.59--dc23
LC record available at http://lccn.loc.gov/2016000308

Super SandCastle™ books are created by a team of professional educators, reading specialists, and content developers around five essential components—phonemic awareness, phonics, vocabulary, text comprehension, and fluency—to assist young readers as they develop reading skills and strategies and increase their general knowledge. All books are written, reviewed, and leveled for guided reading and early reading intervention programs for use in shared, guided, and independent reading and writing activities to support a balanced approach to literacy instruction.

TO ADULT HELPERS

The craft projects in this series are fun and simple. There are just a few things to remember to keep kids safe. Some projects require the use of sharp or hot objects. Also, kids may be using messy materials such as glue or paint. Make sure they protect their clothes and work surfaces. Review the projects before starting, and be ready to assist when necessary.

. . . .

KEY SYMBOL

Watch for this warning symbol in this book. Here is what it means.

 HOT!
You will be working with something hot. Get help from an adult!

CONTENTS

FOREST CRITTERS

A forest is a large area covered with trees. Forests have many critters living in them. Forest critters can be cute. But they are also wild animals. It is best to view them from a safe distance.

To view forest critters close up, craft some! Make small versions of your favorite forest critters right at home.

GET TO KNOW FOREST ANIMALS!

Fun Facts about your favorite forest animals

Foxes

Foxes have **whiskers** on their faces and front legs. They can feel things with their whiskers.

Owls

Owl feathers help them **blend** in with their surroundings. This helps keep them hidden from prey as they hunt.

Bats

Bats are the only **mammals** that can fly. They catch and eat insects while flying.

SKUNKS

Skunks are famous for their stinky spray. It keeps predators away. Skunks can spray up to 10 feet (3 m)!

eagles

Eagles have **amazing** eyes. An eagle can spot a rabbit up to 2 miles (3.2 km) away.

BADGERS

Badgers have strong, sharp claws. They use them to dig for prey. They can dig very fast.

BEARS

Bears have great noses. They can smell food up to 1 mile (1.6 km) away.

moose

Only male moose have antlers. They lose their antlers in the fall. The antlers grow back in the spring.

THREE FOREST LAYERS

Learn about the forest layers and animals

FOREST FLOOR

This layer has soil, dead plants, and small plants. Animals such as moose, foxes, bears, badgers, and skunks live on the forest floor.

canopy

The leaves and branches of trees make up this layer. It can be high in the air! Bats and birds such as eagles and owls live in the canopy.

understory

Small trees and bushes grow in this layer. Moose and bears eat plants in the understory.

9

MATERIALS

HERE ARE SOME OF THE THINGS YOU'LL NEED TO DO THE PROJECTS.

acrylic paint

brown sock

cardboard

chenille stems

craft feathers

craft foam

craft sticks

egg carton

felt

googly eyes

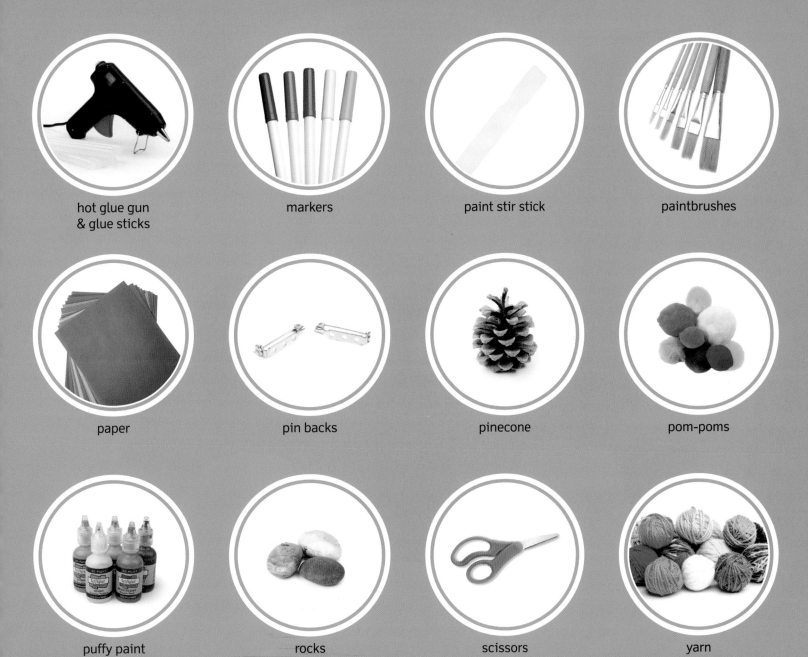

hot glue gun
& glue sticks

markers

paint stir stick

paintbrushes

paper

pin backs

pinecone

pom-poms

puffy paint

rocks

scissors

yarn

BATS SO CUTE

YOU'LL GO BATTY FOR
THIS CRITTER!

MATERIALS 🔥

egg carton	pencil	hot glue gun & glue sticks
scissors	orange yarn	2 googly eyes
black acrylic paint	ruler	
paintbrush	large black pom-pom	

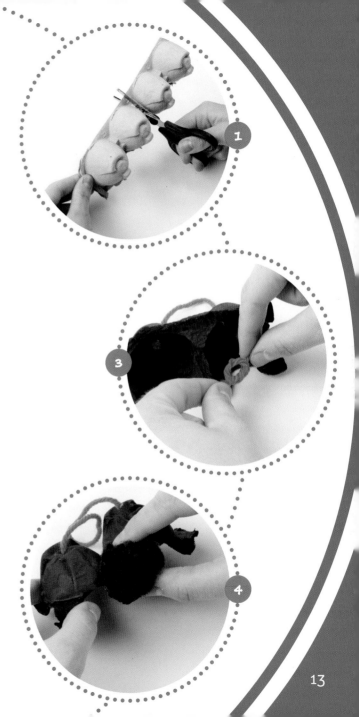

1 Cut two cups off of the egg carton.

2 Paint the egg cups black. Let the paint dry.

3 Use a pencil to poke a hole in the top of each egg cup. Cut a 10-inch (25 cm) piece of yarn. Push one end of the yarn through each hole from the top. Tie a knot in each end of the yarn. The knots must be bigger than the holes.

4 Glue the pom-pom to the front of the egg cups. Center it between the cups. This is the bat's head. Let the glue dry.

5 Glue googly eyes to the pom-pom. Let the glue dry.

6 Use the yarn to hang up your bat.

13

BADGER ME PIN

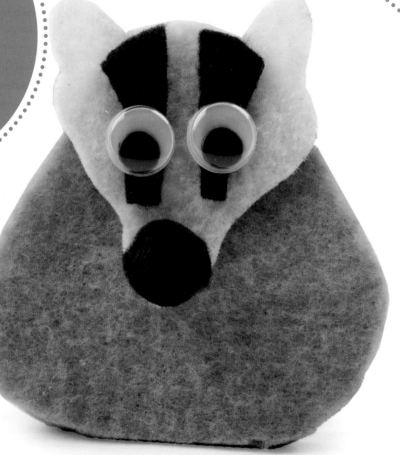

YOU WON'T HAVE TO DIG FOR
THIS CUTE CRITTER!

MATERIALS 🔥

gray, white & black felt   pencil   small black pom-pom
ruler   craft glue   hot glue gun
scissors   marker   & glue sticks
cardboard   2 googly eyes   pin back

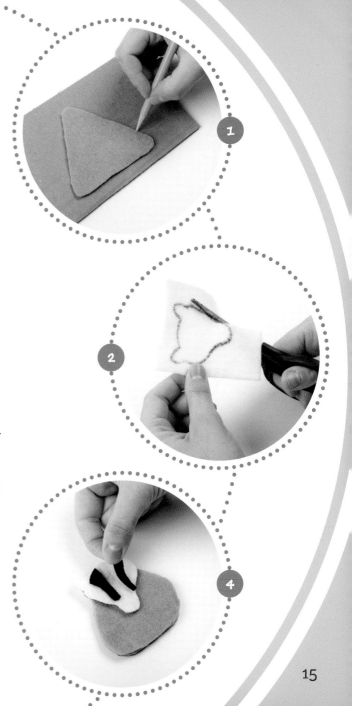

1 Cut a triangle with 4-inch (10 cm) sides out of gray felt. Round the corners off. Trace the shape on the cardboard. Cut out the cardboard shape. Glue the felt triangle to the cardboard triangle.

2 Draw a head shape on white felt. Make it 2 inches (5 cm) high. Include a long nose and two ears. Cut out the head. Glue it over one corner of the felt triangle.

3 Cut two triangles out of black felt. Make them ½ inch (1.3 cm) wide and 1½ inches (4 cm) high. Cut the tips off. Cut the other ends into curves.

4 Lay the black strips on the head. Line the curved ends up with the top of the head. Glue them in place.

5 Glue the googly eyes on top of the black strips. Glue the pom-pom onto the nose.

6 Turn the badger over. Hot glue the pin back to the cardboard. Let the glue dry.

15

CRAZY LIKE A FOX

THIS SLY CRITTER WILL BRIGHTEN YOUR DAY!

orange, white & black
   craft foam
ruler

scissors

craft glue

2 googly eyes

white feather

1.   Cut an oval out of orange craft foam. Make it 4 by 3 inches (10 by 8 cm). Trim the oval so it has a point on one long side. This is the fox's head.

2.   Cut two small ovals out of white foam. Glue them on each side of the point on the head. Trim the edges to match the head.

3.   Cut a small circle out of black foam. This is the nose. Glue it to the point on the head. Glue the googly eyes above the nose.

4.   Cut a rectangle out of orange foam. Make it 3 by 6 inches (7.5 by 15 cm).

5.   Cut an oval out of white foam. Make it a bit smaller than the orange rectangle. Glue the oval in the center of the rectangle. This is the fox's body.

(continued on next page)

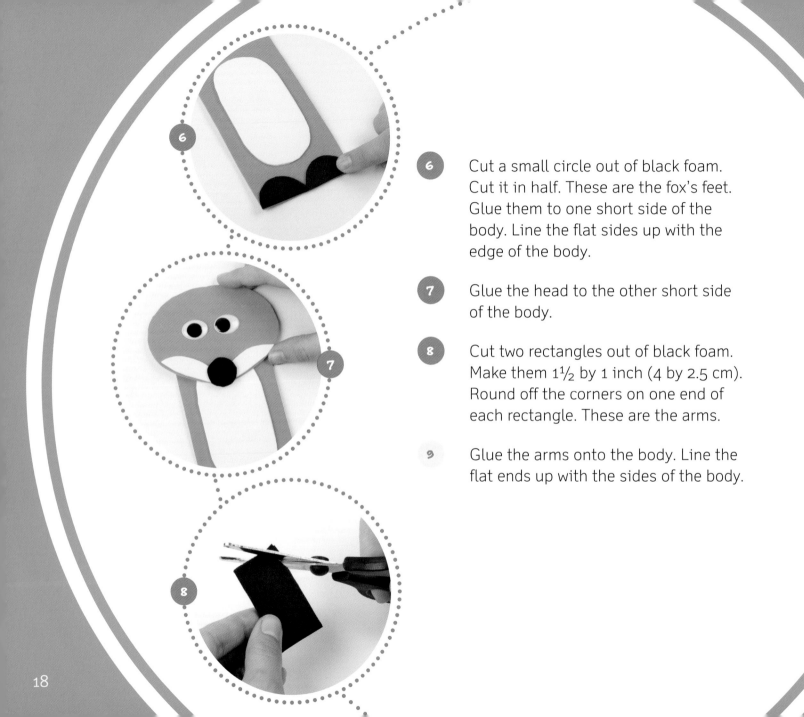

6 Cut a small circle out of black foam. Cut it in half. These are the fox's feet. Glue them to one short side of the body. Line the flat sides up with the edge of the body.

7 Glue the head to the other short side of the body.

8 Cut two rectangles out of black foam. Make them 1½ by 1 inch (4 by 2.5 cm). Round off the corners on one end of each rectangle. These are the arms.

9 Glue the arms onto the body. Line the flat ends up with the sides of the body.

10   Cut two triangles with curved sides out of orange foam. Make them 1½ by 2 inches (4 by 5 cm). These are the ears.

11   Cut two triangles out of white foam. Make them smaller than the orange triangles. Glue them in the center of the ears.

12   Glue the ears behind the top of the head.

13   Cut a long oval with pointed ends out of orange foam. This is the tail.

14   Glue the feather to one end of the tail. Glue the other end of the tail behind the bottom of the body.

MINI CUDDLY SKUNKS

make some sweet skunks
THAT WON'T STINK!

MATERIALS

newspaper

oval rock

black & white
   acrylic paint

paintbrush

black felt

scissors

small white feather

craft glue

2 googly eyes

white chenille stem

1. Cover your work surface with newspaper. Paint the rock black. Let it dry. Paint a white oval or other design on top of the rock. Paint a short white line down the front for the stripe on the face. Paint a small circle on the end for the nose. Let it dry.

2. Cut a teardrop shape out of black felt. Make it a little bigger than the feather. Glue the feather to the felt. This is the tail.

3. Glue a googly eye on each side of the white stripe. Cut two small triangles out of black felt. These are the ears. Glue them behind the eyes.

4. Cut a piece of chenille stem. Glue it to the back of the tail.

5. Glue the other end of the chenille stem to the bottom of the rock. Bend the chenille stem so that the tail sticks up. Let the glue dry.

6. Gather more supplies and make a skunk family!

BEAR IN MIND

THIS BEAR
WILL HELP
DRESS UP
YOUR PENCIL!

MATERIALS

brown chenille stem
scissors
pencil

3 small brown
   pom-poms
puffy paint

large brown pom-pom
craft glue
2 googly eyes

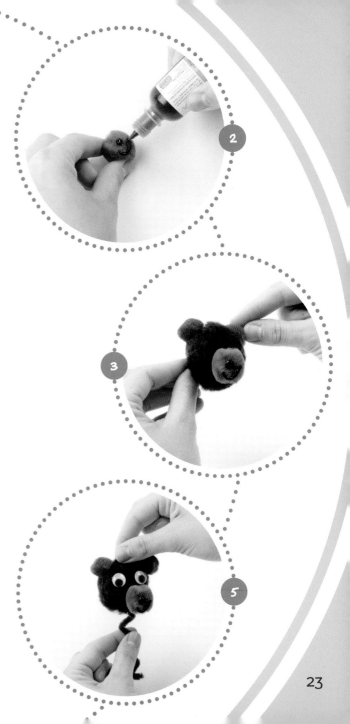

1   Cut the chenille stem in half. Wrap one half around a pencil. Slide it off the pencil.

2   Draw a nose and mouth on a small pom-pom with puffy paint. Glue the small pom-pom to the large pom-pom.

3   Glue two more small pom-poms on top of the large pom-pom. These are the ears.

4   Glue googly eyes between the ears and the nose.

5   Glue the bear head to the end of the curly chenille stem.

6   Slide the chenille stem onto a pen or pencil.

23

HANDSOME FLYING EAGLE

make a regal eagle for your room!

MATERIALS

newspaper

toilet paper tube

white & brown
  acrylic paint

paintbrush

2 googly eyes

craft glue

2 orange chenille stems

scissors

brown paper

pencil

1. Cover your work surface with newspaper. Paint one-fourth of the toilet paper tube white. Paint the rest of the tube brown. Let the paint dry.

2. Glue the googly eyes to the white part of the tube. Cut a chenille stem in half. Roll one half into an oval. Pinch one end into a point to form the beak. Glue it below the eyes.

3. Trace both of your hands on brown paper. Cut out the hand outlines. These are the wings.

4. Cut the second chenille stem in half. Bend one end of each half into an *M* shape. Twist the short end of each *M* around the middle of the stem. These are the feet.

5. Glue the straight ends of the stems inside the tube. The feet should face the front. Bend them up so the eagle can stand on them.

6. Glue a hand on each side of the tube. Bend the hands forward.

SWEET SNOWY OWL

THIS FUZZY OWL
IS A REAL HOOT!

MATERIALS

cotton balls	craft glue	scissors
large pinecone	orange chenille stem	2 googly eyes

1. Pull a few cotton balls into little pieces. Stuff the cotton pieces into the pinecone. Continue until the pinecone is filled with cotton.

2. Glue a cotton ball to the top of the pinecone. This is the head.

3. Cut the chenille stem in half. Roll one half into an oval. Fold the oval in half. Pinch the ends into points. This is the beak. Glue it onto the head.

4. Glue the googly eyes above the beak. Let the glue dry.

MIGHTY MOOSE PUPPET

MOOSE UP YOUR LIFE WITH THIS SOCK PUPPET!

28

MATERIALS

brown & off-white felt
scissors
brown sock
paper
pencil

ruler
black & brown markers
newspaper
craft glue
craft stick

2 small brown pom-poms
2 googly eyes
paint stir stick

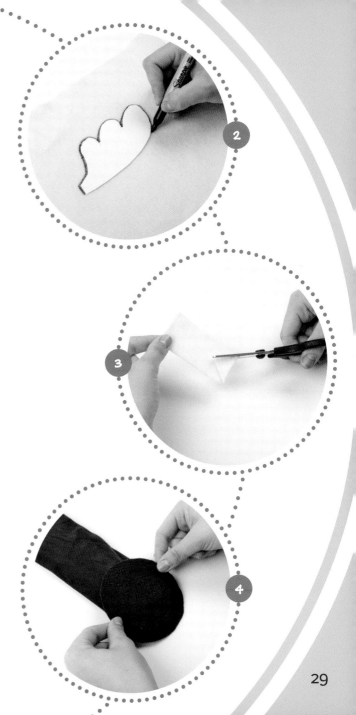

1. Cut a circle out of brown felt. Make it slightly bigger than the width of the sock.

2. Draw a moose antler on a piece of paper. Make it at least 4 inches (10 cm) long. Cut it out. Trace the antler shape two times on off-white felt. Cut out the antlers.

3. Cut two rectangles out of off-white felt. Make them 3 by 1½ inches (7.5 by 4 cm). These are the legs. Cut a triangle out of one end of each leg. These are the hooves. Color the hooves with a brown marker.

4. Put a few layers of newspaper inside the sock, all the way to the toe. This will keep the glue from sticking the sides together. Glue the felt circle over the toe of the sock.

(continued on next page)

5 Turn the sock over. Glue the legs to the sock on each side of the felt circle.

6 Glue the antlers about 1 inch (2.5 cm) away from the legs. Make sure the antler's bumps point away from the legs.

7 Glue the craft stick across the antlers.

8. Turn the sock back over. Glue the small pom-poms to the felt circle for **nostrils**.

9. Glue the googly eyes above the felt circle. Let the glue dry.

10. Remove the newspaper from inside the sock. Fold the moose head down so that it bends just above the antlers.

11. Stick the paint stir stick into the sock. Push it up to the fold. Glue the stick in place. Let the glue dry.

GLOSSARY

amazing – wonderful or surprising.

blend – to match the surrounding environment.

mammal – a warm-blooded animal that has hair and whose females produce milk to feed their young.

nostril – an opening in the nose.

whisker – one of the long hairs around the mouth of an animal.